Frontier Village

A Town Is Born

by Catherine E. Chambers
illustrated by Dick Smolinski

Will knew it was going to happen. As soon as the Nesbitts moved into their log house in 1848, Ma started pestering Pa about a school. "You promised me we'd settle near a school, Martin Nesbitt! You know how important education is!"

The nearest school in Wisconsin was across the river, many miles away.

"We'll do something about it, Evie," Pa said. "There will be other families settling here soon. Then we can build a school—or maybe a footbridge across the river."

"You'd better," Ma said. Her dark eyes snapped. "Our children aren't going to grow up ignorant!"

Will thought he was safe from books that winter. There was ice on the river. Pa had a lot of work to do making furniture for the new cabin. The animals needed tending. It was too late now to start building a bridge.

Ma saw Will grin. "Don't count your chickens before they're hatched, young man. I brought my old school books with us in the wagon. You and your sisters are going to go to school right here!"

That winter Ma gave them lessons by propping a book in front of the washtub while she scrubbed clothes. Will found smooth dark stones that Jessie and Eliza could use for slates. Pa gave Will arithmetic problems like this one to do: "If our chickens eat three cups of grain a day, how many bushels of grain do we need to last till spring?"

Pa was worried about having enough grain. Their first real crop wouldn't come until next summer. Pa did some logging work for Mr. Beecher, their nearest neighbor, in return for some wheat and corn. But both men wished there was a store where they could buy and sell goods. The nearest store was two days' ride away.

Mrs. Beecher wished for a church. "We have family prayers, but it's not the same as getting together on Sundays with other folks."

Everybody agreed. Life on the frontier could be wonderful. But they wished they were closer to a town.

All over the western territories, it was the same. As soon as explorers and trappers spread the news of rich lands and opportunity, pioneers came. And soon after homesteads were carved out of the wilderness, towns would spring up.

Towns were started in many ways. Some were begun by men who had dreams of founding towns named after them. Some towns sprang up by themselves, just where they were needed. They grew and bloomed like sagebrush ...on river banks, where trails crossed, where Indian tribes held councils. These were all places easy for travelers to reach.

A town might begin as a crossroads. Then it might become a settlement, then a town. Certain towns started when the United States Government put territory land on sale. Some people bought up large sections of it. Then the landowners advertised for settlers. They tried to attract craftsmen whose skills would be needed in the new towns.

Sometimes an entire village in the States would decide to move west. Some family members might be too old or feeble to make the trip. There were many sad good-byes, because no one knew if they would meet again. The neighbors would travel together in a wagon train, helping one another. When they reached an area they all liked, they would settle within a few miles of each other. That way, the new life was not so hard and strange.

Other towns grew slowly, like the one near the Nesbitts and the Beechers. That first spring, Mrs. Nesbitt gave both the Nesbitt and the Beecher children their lessons. The summer that Will Nesbitt and Jake Beecher were ten, their fathers built a footbridge across the river. Now the children could walk to school. When the bridge broke, they waded through the water. In the winter they slid across the ice. They left home at dawn and got back after dark. The next spring, Jessie got caught in quicksand. It took both Pa and Mr. Beecher to get her out.

Ma stamped her foot. "That settles it! Next year we're building ourselves a school!"

Before spring was over, Mrs. Beecher came to the Nesbitts' house and announced, "We've a new family half an hour away—the Andersons. And Mr. Anderson is a preacher!"

Robert Anderson was a minister and a farmer. His daughter Lucy was sixteen. She had a certificate saying she had graduated from a school in Kentucky. Mrs. Anderson hung the certificate on her cabin wall, and Mrs. Nesbitt and Mrs. Beecher saw it when they went to visit. It said Lucy had studied arithmetic, bookkeeping, civil government, grammar, and composition. She had also studied drawing, geography, history, penmanship, physiology, botany, and the art of teaching. Mrs. Beecher and Mrs. Nesbitt looked at each other. It didn't take them long to decide they had found a teacher for their school.

During the summer, the men added a small room to the Anderson cabin. In September, Lucy started teaching school to twenty pupils.

In Miss Lucy's classroom, children sat on backless benches. Girls were on one side of the aisle, and boys on the other. Will sat towards the back, because he was one of the older students. The six-year-olds were in the front. Miss Lucy hung pictures on the walls. She made charts of numbers for the little ones to copy. She made penmanship charts in her beautiful handwriting. Will and the others practiced copying them on their slates. Children without slates traced their lessons with their fingers in a sandbox.

There were few books to study. Miss Lucy had a primer, or "first reader," from which she taught the youngest children their ABC's. Mr. Anderson sent to Chicago for some hornbooks. A hornbook was a wooden paddle with a piece of paper pasted to it. Upon the paper, proverbs were written. The paper was protected by a clear sheet of horn. Later, the parents bought a set of McGuffey's Readers. These were the most famous school books of the nineteenth century. All the readings in a book

were at the same level. When a child finished reading at
one "grade," he or she went on to the next. Because classes
were all given in one room, a child could be in third-grade
arithmetic and fourth-grade geography at the same time.
Will found that after his mother's lessons, he was a sixth-
grade reader. But he was only at fourth grade in arithmetic, just like his sister Jessie.

When Miss Lucy called out "Sixth-grade reading," Will and Jake Beecher and Sarah Cummings went up front. They stood in a line and read aloud from their readers. Each of them read a paragraph in turn until they had finished their lesson for the day. After that, Miss Lucy asked them to take the second graders to the back of the

room and hear their reading lesson. While they did this, Miss Lucy asked the fourth graders history questions. That way, every child recited aloud in all subjects. When they weren't reciting, they did work with their slates or books, or helped each other.

Will learned to memorize well and to do arithmetic problems in his head. He memorized poetry and parts of the Constitution. He wanted to do well because in spring there would be a special day when they would recite aloud before their parents. Besides, learning was fun—it was often like a game.

"Boys against girls," Miss Lucy would say. "Arithmetic. Who can tell me first what is 6,537 times 2,817?" The day Will finally won the arithmetic contest he went home grinning from ear to ear.

At noon Miss Lucy rang a brass bell for recess. All the children took their lunch baskets outdoors in good weather. It was fun to sit under a tree and eat with friends. Afterwards there was time to play games like tug of war or tag. Sometimes Miss Lucy played, too. On Friday afternoons, there was always a "spell-down," or spelling bee.

School ended in late spring. Boys and girls were needed to work at home during the farming season. In the summer of 1852, when Will was thirteen, five more families came to the area. That meant more children. Just before harvest time, the men got together and built a schoolhouse big enough to hold all the students. They built it at the crossroads where the trails between all the cabins met. There still was just one classroom. But there was a cloakroom with hooks for shawls and jackets and a shelf for lunch baskets. There was a desk for Miss Lucy. On the girls' side of the room was a chimney and a shiny Franklin stove. This helped keep heat in the room instead of letting it escape up the chimney. Even so, the girls became too warm while the boys shivered. So Miss Lucy made them change places after lunch each day.

Some people thought Miss Lucy was very young to be a teacher. But Will and Jake knew she was strict even if she was young. They learned that lesson the day they had a fight during noon recess. Miss Lucy made them apologize, and they spent the afternoon standing in opposite corners of the room. Then she made them write "I will not fight" a hundred times.

14

Now that the school was built, the Reverend Robert Anderson told the men it was time to build a church. Ma and Mrs. Beecher and the other women had made up their minds about that already. Mr. Anderson farmed on weekdays like the other men. But on Sunday he put on his black coat and broad-brimmed hat and "rode round the district." Each Sunday, he held services at a different home, and the neighbors who lived closest always came.

One Sunday, services were being held at the Nesbitt home. "Getting to be a whole lot of families out here now," Pa said. He looked around the cabin at all the folks who had come. "I've been thinking, Evie. Our farm's doing well. Will's almost a man and does a fine job helping me. The crops don't take all my time, especially in winter. I might dam up the stream and build us a sawmill. You know how many of the new folks trade with me for the wood they need. My brother Dan's been writing how much he likes the sound of life out here. He's been working in his father-in-law's store in Ohio. Maybe he'd like to start a store here."

"Oh, you just want this crossing to be named Nesbittville," Ma teased. But she liked the idea herself.

A town was ready to be born. From the beginning, folks had missed things they took for granted back home —a church, a school, a store where they could buy or trade for the things they didn't make. Having to do so many things for themselves took their time from the things that they did best. There were now enough people in and near the crossing to support a cobbler and a blacksmith and a tanner.

17

Late that spring a wagon train rattled through the crossing. When Miss Lucy heard it coming, she let all the children run outside to watch. The wagons stopped. A young man in a fine suit of clothes stepped down. "Can you tell me how I can find the Nesbitt place?" he asked. It was Will's Uncle Dan, come west with his bride to start a general store!

All the wagon-train families stayed with families from the crossing that night. Uncle Dan and Aunt Catherine sat up late talking excitedly with the Nesbitts. A brawny blacksmith and his family stayed with the Beechers. The wagon train stayed through Sunday. That afternoon, everyone gathered at the Beecher cabin. As the women unpacked the dinners they'd brought, Will and Jake ran outside.

"My uncle's going to buy some land near the crossing and start a store. And I'm going to help him," Will bragged. "I'll help my Pa, too. Pa's going to put up a sawmill. They planned it all last night."

"Well, I'm going to help Blacksmith Brown," Jake answered. "He's decided to stay here, too. He said I'm so big and strong he'd take me on as an apprentice if I wanted."

This was how craftsmen learned their trades, by helping their parents or by apprenticing themselves to a skilled craftsman. That meant the apprentice promised to work for the craftsman, usually for seven years. He was given little or no pay, but he received food and clothes and a place to sleep, while he learned a trade.

19

Many things happened at the crossing that summer! There was a church-raising, just as there had been "raisings" to build people's cabins and for the school. For three days all the families in the area gathered and helped. And when they weren't planting their crops, they helped Uncle Dan raise his house. The walls were made of clapboard instead of logs, and the building was two stories high. Downstairs was the store, and Uncle Dan and Aunt Catherine lived above it. Pa built his sawmill, too. It was

great fun damming up the stream, even though Ma didn't think much of the mud the children brought home.

By September, folks were saying, "I'm going to Nesbitt's," when they meant they were going to the sawmill or the store. So soon the town had a name—Nesbitt's Crossing! By October, the blacksmith's forge was blazing in the lean-to behind the Brown's new cabin. And Miss Lucy Anderson got engaged to a young farmer who'd come with the wagon train.

"We'll be needing a new teacher in another year if Miss Lucy doesn't stay on," Ma said. "Maybe Will could take the job." Boys and girls who had been bright students often became teachers as soon as they completed studying in the local schoolhouse. Teachers were paid ten to fourteen dollars a month, and often "boarded round." That meant they stayed with a different family every month. Meals and lodging were considered part of the teacher's salary. Will wouldn't have to board round if he taught. But he wasn't sure if teaching was for him. He thought he might like to go into business with Uncle Dan in the general-merchandise store.

Country stores could be exciting places! Uncle Dan said he aimed to have everything folks needed "from the cradle to the grave." Shelves held bolts of fabric. There were medicines and cooking needs. There were barrels of nails and packets of bright-colored dyes. Now women no longer had to make all their dyes from herbs and grasses and vegetable skins. There were barrels of sugar and crackers, tea and coffee. There were felt hats. There were rifles. There were spices from faraway places—pepper,

cinnamon, nutmeg, and cloves. All these were bought by Uncle Dan from well-dressed young salesmen who came through Nesbitt's Crossing on their selling routes. The salesmen brought with them news of the big cities and plenty of gossip and funny stories.

The general store was a popular meeting place for the people of the town. After school and all day Saturdays, Will helped his uncle. He learned to wait patiently while customers decided what they wanted. He learned how to tell the value of things taken in trade and how to keep neat records in the ledger book. He was glad he had done well in arithmetic! He liked hearing the salesmen's stories. But best of all, he liked the days when big freight wagons full of new supplies pulled into town. A freight wagon was a huge wagon, pulled by six horses. It had a canvas top hooped and drawn in with ropes. Will could hear the horses' hoofs pounding the earth even before he saw the wagon through clouds of dust. As the wagon pulled in, all the dogs barked. The hens fluttered out of the way. It seemed like everybody in Nesbitt's Crossing just happened to come around the day a freighter arrived!

Everyone came the days the post rider delivered the mail sack, too. Uncle Dan fixed part of his store as a post office. Folks paid about twenty-five cents for each page of a letter.

Nesbitt's Crossing was growing fast. There was law in the little town now. Mr. Brown, the blacksmith, was made a sheriff. If he needed, he could appoint other men as deputies to help him. But there wasn't often trouble. Every month or so a circuit rider came through town. He was a judge who "rode the circuit" between frontier towns in the Territory, setting up court wherever need be.

Other craftsmen came to Nesbitt's Crossing. Near Pa's sawmill, a miller set up his water wheel and gristmill. Folks brought their wheat and rye there to be ground. Usually, they paid the miller with some flour. Not far away was a tanner and a cooper who made barrels, pails, and washtubs. Jake Beecher spent every moment he could at the blacksmith's. All the boys liked hanging around the forge as much as their little brothers and sisters liked hanging around the penny candy at the store.

In June, Will and Jake both graduated from school. Miss Lucy told Will he was a good enough scholar to go on to an academy if he wanted. That was a special school for young men and women, where students could continue their education. "Or you could teach right now," Miss Lucy said. "You can be very proud of how well you've done. Your diploma shows you could be a fine teacher."

Will was very pleased with Miss Lucy's praise. But he wasn't sure if he wanted to be a teacher. The idea of going into business with Uncle Dan still appealed to him.

So many decisions lay before him. But whatever Will decided, he knew there was a future for him in Nesbitt's Crossing. The land was still frontier. But in a few years Will had seen it grow from wilderness to a little town. It would grow further, and he was determined to be part of it!

Index

*(Page numbers that appear in **boldface** type refer to illustrations.)*

academy, for continued education, 29
apprentice, to craftsman, 19
arithmetic, 4, 9, 11, 13, 25

barrels, **16**, 22, **23**, 29, **29**
blacksmith, 17, 19, **19**, 21, 26, 29
"boarding round," 22
bookkeeping, 9
books, 3, 4, 10, **11**, 13; *see also* readers
botany, 9
bridge, *see* footbridge

cabins, 3, **3**, **5**, 10, 14, 17, 20, 21
certificate, teaching, 9
chickens, 4, **24**, 25
church, 5, 15, **15**, 17
    raising of, 20
cinnamon, 23
circuit rider, 26
cities, news from, 23
civil government, 9
clapboard, 20
classroom, 10, **11**, 14
cloakroom, 14
cloves, 23
cobbler, 17
coffee, 22
composition, 9
Constitution, the, 13
cooper, 29, **29**
corn, 5
court, 26, **27**
crackers, 22
craftsmen, 19, 29
    need for, 6
crops, 5, 17, 20
crossing, 17, 18, 19, 20
crossroads, 6, 14
    see also crossing

deputies, 26
diploma, 29
dogs, **24**, 25
drawing, 9
dyes, 22

explorers, 5

fabric, 22
farming, 9, 15, 17, 21
    children's help needed for, 14
"first reader," *see* primer
flour, 29
footbridge, 3, 8
    building of, **8**
forge, **19**, 21, 29
Franklin stove, 14
freight wagons, **24**, 25

frontier, 5, 30
furniture making, **2**, 3

games, 13
general store, *see* store
geography, 9, 11
gossip, 23
grain, 4, 5
grammar, 9
gristmill, 29

hats, 22
hens, *see* chickens
history, 9, 13
homesteads, 5
hornbook, 10, **10**
horses, **24**, 25, **26**

Indian tribes, 6

judge, 26, **27**

landowners, 6
lean-to, 21
ledger book, 25
lessons, 4, 8, 12, 13
logs, 3, 5, **5**, 20
lunch baskets, 13, 14

mail, 26
McGuffey's Readers, 10
medicines, 22
memorizing, 13
miller, 29
minister, 9
    holding services, 15, 17, **17**

nails, 22
nutmeg, 23

Ohio, 17

pails, 29
penmanship, 9, 10
penny candy, 29
pepper, 22
physiology, 9
pioneers, 5
poetry, 13
post office, 26
post rider, 26, **26**
preacher, *see* minister
primer, 10

quicksand, 9

"raisings," of buildings, 20
readers, 10, 12, **12**
reading lesson, 12, 13
recess, 13, 14

reciting, 13
"riding the circuit," 26
rifles, 22
river, 3, 6, 8, **8**
rye, 29

sandbox, 10
sawmill, 17, 19, 20, 21, 29
school, 3, 8, 9, 10, 17, 20, 25, 29
    see also classroom
schoolhouse, 22
    design of, 14
services, church, 15, 17, **17**
settlement, 6
settlers, 6
sheriff, 26, **27**
slates, 4, 10, 13
"spell-down," *see* spelling bee
spelling bee, 13
spices, 22
spring, 4, 8, 9, 13, 14, 18
store, 5, 17, 18, 19, 20, 21, **22**, 25, **25**, 29
    goods sold at, 22
    salesmen visiting, 22, **23**, 25
sugar, 22
summer, 5, 8, 10, 14, 20

tag, 13
tanner, 17, 29
tea, 22
teacher, 9, 14, 29, 30
    payment of, 22
territories, western, 5, 26
territory land, sale of, 6
towns, 5, 8, 26, 30
    beginning of, 5, 6
    growth of, 17, 26
    location of, 6
    naming of, 6, 17, 21
trade, 17, 19, 25
trails, 6, 14
trappers, 5
tug of war, 13

United States Goverment, 6

village, relocation of, 6

wagon, 3, **7**, 18, **18**, 21; *see also* freight wagons
wagon train, 6, **7**, 18, 19, 21
washtub, 4, **4**, 29
water wheel, 29
wheat, 5, 29
wilderness, 5, 30
winter, 3, 9, 17
Wisconsin, 3

This edition published 1999 by Troll Communications L.L.C.

Printed in the United States of America.

10   9   8   7   6   5   4   3   2   1

Cover art by Robert F. Goetzl.

Library of Congress Cataloging-in-Publication Data

Chambers, Catherine E.
     Frontier village.

     (Adventures in frontier America)
     Summary: Recounts the growth of the town of Nesbitt's
Crossing from the time the first settlers, the Nesbitt
family, came to that area of Wisconsin in 1848.
     [1. Frontier and pioneer life—Wisconsin—Fiction.]
I. Smolinski, Dick, ill.   II. Title.   III. Series:
Chambers, Catherine E. Adventures in frontier America.
PZ7.C3558Frp   1984   [Fic]   83-18271
ISBN 0-8167-0045-1 (lib. bdg.)
ISBN 0-8167-5040-8 (pbk.)